THE MOJO AND THE SAYSO

Aishah Rahman

BROADWAY PLAY PUBLISHING INC
224 E 62nd St, NY, NY 10065
www.broadwayplaypub.com
info@broadwayplaypub.com

THE MOJO AND THE SAYSO
© Copyright 1989 by Aishah Rahman

First published in an acting edition by B P P I in August 1990
First printing this edition: November 2010
I S B N: 978-0-88145-462-8

Book design: Marie Donovan
Typographic controls & page make-up: Adobe InDesign
Typeface: Palatino
Printed and bound in the U S A

INTRODUCTION:
MAKING THE MUSIC OF LIFE

Aishah Rahman's writing is synonymous with music.
Her plays LADY DAY: A MUSICAL TRAGEDY,
TRANSCENDENTAL BLUES, THE LADY AND THE
TRAMP, THE TALE OF MADAME ZORA, along
with the three plays collected here—UNFINISHED
WOMEN CRY IN NO MAN'S LAND WHILE A BIRD
DIES IN A GILDED CAGE, THE MOJO AND THE
SAYSO, and ONLY IN AMERICA—reverberate with
musical form, sound, and power. Her elegant writing
creates the music of life—music and life at once racial
and beyond race, at once gendered and beyond gender,
at once spatial and beyond space. Her eloquent plays
take place at the intersection of the finely crafted and
spirited improvisational, at the intersection where the
visually extraordinary and invisible everydayness
meet. Making the invisible music of life visible is no
easy task, but Aishah Rahman makes it appear an
effortless feast of sounds. She is a high priestess of
wisdom and words conjuring magic spells for people
to hear their dreams, see their possibilities, and know
their better selves. She weaves spells of transformation
and hope, of continuity and love, perhaps especially
of love—of self as well as of family and community—
for all human kind besieged by violence and pain, by
disappointment and confusion, by oppression and
isolation. In rhythmic, jazz-rooted language and mosaic

dramatic structures, she meditates on the power of the
spirit within to live, and to do so despite debilitating
material conditions and absurd social conditions, or
corrupt institutions and fractured psyches. Although
she works the magic of words to reconstitute a
personal self within the transformative energy of
communal voice, she speaks from an outsider position,
one ever observant and knowledgeable of what human
beings do to one another. It is from this location of
herself that Aishah Rahman actively engages in the
dangerous work of securing the ground for a collective
future.

UNFINISHED WOMEN CRY IN NO MAN'S
LAND WHILE A BIRD DIES IN A GILDED CAGE,
the first of the plays collected here, has become an
"underground classic," much performed and often
discussed in college and community theaters, because
its polydramatic form fused with music has powerful
resonance above ground. Once seen, it is a play one
does not soon forget. Its simultaneous subjects are the
pregnant residents of a 1950s home for unwed mothers
and the innovative saxophonist "Bird," Charlie Parker.
While Bird's music and his inventive genius infuse the
stage with creative life, his final hours in his mistress's
boudoir visually confront the issues of death, loss,
unfulfillment. Synchronically, the girl-women of the
Hide-a-Wee Home, already in the late stages of their
pregnancies, must decide the fate of their babies, and
in the process of making that momentous decision they
confront the realities of their own lives and aloneness.
In UNFINISHED WOMEN CRY IN NO MAN'S
LAND WHILE A BIRD DIES IN A GILDED CAGE,
as Margaret Wilkerson has said, Aishah Rahman
"reaches beyond statistics and sociological theories
to find the unarticulated, half-understood longings of
teenage mothers." Music provides the connective link

that makes understanding possible. One of the girl-women links her inner world to the creative expression possible in music: "It's only in the head of a musician that I begin to understand. Only a musician can make sense of me. Only a musician knows how to connect...." Indeed, Bird's playing, heard throughout the drama, connects the subjects of life and death, of wholeness and fragmentation, of community and isolation. It communicates the otherwise inarticulate through the sound and language of music. Wilma, who is about to give birth, recalls her life through Bird's music: "Charlie Parker played in tongues.... S'funny what Bird means to me. Secretly, I always wanted to be a man `cause they can do things and go places. Bird is the man I wanted to be." Wilma, like her sister residents, is trapped both by the limited possibilities and gender roles society offers women and by the overwhelming physical and emotional needs that mark the female body as vulnerable to the promise of connection and tenderness in sexual intercourse. Nevertheless, Wilma manages to sing: "O lovely music man/Women want you for your energy/Many love you for your song/ The whole universe/swings to your melodies/And everybody will listen/When I shout.... Bird Lives, Bird Lives, Bird Lives!" Her insistence on life and music complicates any attempt to consign these characters to the realm of tragedy.

In THE MOJO AND THE SAYSO, the second of the plays in this collection, the domestic space of Acts and Awilda Benjamin functions as a symbolic landscape of ritual and magic. Within this surreal place individuals have a "sayso," the voice of personal empowerment so necessary in a world that would dehumanize and demonize those without the power of words. Aishah Rahman traces the origin and conception of THE MOJO AND THE SAYSO to a 1970s case of mistaken

identity and police brutality when a policeman shot
and killed Clifford Glover, a ten-year-old boy who
was out walking with his father. She has recalled that
the Glover family's story compelled her to write the
play: "I knew that the family were people who were
voiceless. And I had to give voice to them." Their need
to speak their tragedy and her own need to counter
senseless violence provide the occasion for the rituals
of survival and transcendence in THE MOJO AND
THE SAYSO. This play, a reality-defying absurdist
romp, has also provided the occasion for Aishah
Rahman to reflect on her work and to describe her
art as crafted out of a "jazz aesthetic," the tradition of
articulating the multiplicity of conscious experiences
and the various levels of reality coexistent in any given
moment in an individual's life. THE MOJO AND
THE SAYSO represents the language capable of such
multilayered expression as instrumental solos, and
the scenes enacting the possibility of triumph over
adversity and sorrow as a surrealistic fantasy in which
voice, actualized and materialized as Sayso, projects
magical power.

To be a sayer and a seer in these times, however, is to
be a risk-taker. ONLY IN AMERICA, the last of the
plays collected here, is a powerful signing of the full-
visioned playwright: self-confident, iconoclastic, and
daring. The risks are evident in the play's sacrilegious
humor and scathing satire, which hold no icons
sacred, yet surround human beings in the laughter
of love and delight, in the knowledge that words and
lives matter. Written in the aftermath of the televised
Clarence Thomas-Anita Hill Senate hearings, ONLY
IN AMERICA engages politics and gender in an
admixture of the seriousness of musical composition
and the playfulness of word games. The satirical take
on political absurdities is deftly humorous, but the

characters' speech is not the language of laughter: Cassandra, who understands words and language but cannot speak coherent words; Oral, who heads the Animal Bureau of Civil Rights, but laughs his hatred of animals; ScatWoman, who cleans by sprinkling dust, "Catching dirt with dirt," and singing "shoo be doo do"; and Lilli, whose motto is "A silent woman is a defenseless woman." Wildly farcical and wickedly satirical, the movement to empowerment through speech coalesces in the final ringing command: "Speak out!" ONLY IN AMERICA reminds us that Aishah Rahman's project from the beginning has been making the invisible visible, making the voices of the silent heard, making the music of new languages, and moving beyond old boundaries and categories of expression.

Mention the name "Aishah Rahman," and the response of anyone interested in plays and the theater is not "Aishah who?" but an instantaneous "I love her plays." Audiences may love her plays, but commercial theaters have been slow to produce them. Aishah Rahman has labeled this phenomenon her "Not for Our Theater Stamp of Disapproval." Yet her own joyful love affair with drama has indeed spilled over to audiences, actors, playwrights, and now—with this collection—new audiences will have access to her work. Sydne Mahone, in *Moon marked and touched by the sun*, links Aishah Rahman with Adrienne Kennedy and Ntozake Shange as "the first generation of stylistic rebels" who have reached "maturity as playwrights" and "held the ground for black women playwrights, steadily singin' `I Shall Not Be Moved,' all the while movin' mountains." This assessment seems appropriate for a remarkable and visionary playwright who is one of a very few African-American women to achieve a recognized status in contemporary drama.

In fact, there are only a very few dramatists who come immediately to mind when thinking about the major contemporary African-American playwrights: Lorraine Hansberry, LeRoi Jones (Amiri Baraka), Adrienne Kennedy, August Wilson, Ntozake Shange, and Aishah Rahman. Although she has not had the general name recognition of her contemporaries, Aishah Rahman has been widely celebrated for the craft, language, and vision of her plays. Her daring, innovative fusion of form and function has positioned her in the forefront of American women writing for the theater, and in the forefront of those playwrights who expand the limits, refuse the boundaries, and seek new territories in the formal and stylistic properties of drama as a genre and the theater as a medium. The transformative power of her vision helps us to know that the world of drama is alive, alert, and attuned to this late twentieth-century moment and to a Sybil who will not let us escape the piercing staccato of her riffs or the lyrical reaches of her arias.

With the availability of the three plays in this text, Aishah Rahman's work and her achievement will become better known by students of the American theater. Iconoclastic, but never preachy or bombastic, these collected plays break through the arbitrary boundaries that would contain and crush the human spirit into categories that hide the shape and the essence of being alive. In the multiplicity of her musical and aesthetic tastes, as well as in the richness of her perceptive and inspired language, Aishah Rahman calls for transformation and change through revisioning the past and rewriting the future. Her work is a gift to us: a lifeline of words and images, a lifeline that helps us traverse a sometimes murky, always complex terrain and that enables us to find our own way, empowered and enspirited. These are plays for today. These are plays for the ages. The melodies are magical. The words are magical melodies—awaiting our hearing. These are plays that keep the stage alive with the hope and the freedom of human creativity. These are plays we dare not ignore.

Thadious M Davis
Gertrude Conaway Vanderbilt Professor of English
Vanderbilt University

ORIGINAL PRODUCTION

THE MOJO AND THE SAYSO was originally produced by the Crossroads Theatre Company in New Brunswick, NJ, which presented the play from 9 November through 4 December 1988. The cast and creative contributors were:

AWILDA ....Stephanie Berry
ACTS..Matthew Idason
BLOOD.. Victor Mack
PASTOR .... Gregory Daniel

Director... George Ferencz
Set designer..Bill Stabile
Costumes... Sally J Lesser
Lighting...Blu
Sound .... Rob Gorton

CHARACTERS & SETTING

AWILDA
ACTS
BLOOD
PASTOR

Time: Now. Sunday.

Place: The living room of the Benjamins' home.

PLAYWRIGHT'S NOTE

THE MOJO AND THE SAYSO is a story of a family: vulnerable human beings who sustain pain and love, hatreds, fears, joys, sorrows, and degradation, and finally triumph.

This play is not conceived or written in a naturalistic mode. Therefore, the directing style should serve the absurdity, fantasy, and magical mayhem that are intrinsic to the script. The monologues in the play are conceived as jazz solos. In each monologue the actor's speech is conceived as a riff on a specific instrument (the director is free to choose which instrument), and both body movements and speech are rooted in classical jazz rhythms.

for George Jackson, Clifford Glover, and all the
Others...

For he that survives, for he whose spirits flourish
For he who be corralled, mashed up, downpressed
Many waters cannot quench he
Neither can the floods him drown
His gentle name be written in the whirlwind.

ACT ONE

(Morning. Lights up on the Benjamins' living room. Stage left is a mantelpiece with a collection of various colored candles on it. Center stage, on a slightly raised platform, is a half-built car. Hubcaps, tires, fenders, etc. are scattered around. The rest of the room is neat; it is only the platform area that is disordered. AWILDA, dressed entirely in white, is frantically searching for something among the mechanical automotive parts. Her voice is heard over the whirr of an acetylene torch which ACTS, inside the car frame, is using.)

AWILDA: *(Searching frantically for something very important)* Ball joints, tires, shock absorbers, spark plugs, carburetors.

ACTS: The treasures and dreams that's buried in a junkyard!

(AWILDA stares at him unbelievingly for a second, then continues her search.)

ACTS: Damn near tore my paws off trying to get to this baby but I got it. Knowed it was only a few left in the world. Never thought I'd own one but I do now. A Lycoming engine. They used to put it in only the best of machines back in '47. Used to put it in a deluxe car they called the Auborn Cord. It had an electric shift, front-wheel drive same as you got today. Car was so advanced, so ahead of its time, they took it off the market. Man this engine was so bad they used to put her in aeroplanes. Now I'm gonna put her right in, Jim!

AWILDA: Wrenches, hammers.

ACTS: Soon I'll be finished the dream car of my mind.

AWILDA: *(Reacts to his last words by looking at him and shaking her head; she resumes her search.)* Batteries, mufflers, spark coils, piston rings, radiator caps, gaskets, fenders, exhaust pipes. White gloves? No white gloves.

ACTS: A chrome-plated masterpiece. Brown and gold-flecked with a classy body...built with my own hands.

AWILDA: I can't find them.

(ACTS' only response is to continue working.)

AWILDA: I searched and looked and searched and still can't find them. I searched and looked and rummaged all through this mess and I still can't.... *(Going to the mantelpiece)* Let's see. Orange. A good color for concentration. *(She lights the candle and is immediately soothed.)* There. I've lit the way to my white gloves. I'll have them in time to go to church.

(ACTS' only response is to bang with his hammer.)

AWILDA: Pastor Delroy wants all us saints dressed in white. Pure white, from crown to toe.

ACTS: What a beautiful engine. They don't come any better.

AWILDA: Don't forget this Sunday is special.

ACTS: A priceless engine. Tossed away in the junkyard.

AWILDA: It happened three years ago today.

ACTS: Been looking for this engine for three years.

AWILDA: And Pastor is having a special memorial service today for Linus.

ACTS: And what do you know? Boom! This morning out of all the hundreds of other mornings. This is the morning I find him.

AWILDA: There's gonna be organ music.

ACTS: Must be some kind of special sign...finding this engine this morning.

AWILDA: And flowers. Gladiolas and carnations. Lovely church flowers.

ACTS: Now that I got the engine I want, I can finish him. Finish him today. Three years is a long time.

AWILDA: Our choir will sing *Sweet Lil' Jesus Boy*.

ACTS: Soon he'll be purring like a kitten. Soon every nut and bolt will be in place.

AWILDA: And the congregation will bow their heads for a moment of silence. And think of Linus.

ACTS: Shut up! I see no need to draw attention to the unfortunate byproducts of your womb!

AWILDA: Our children. What became of our children?

ACTS: *(Getting up suddenly and leaving the room)* We'll say no more about it. No more!

AWILDA: *(Hurling these words at his exiting back)* You never talk about anything! Especially not about Linus.

ACTS: *(Returns, carrying a steering wheel)* That's another thing. He's dead. Let the dead rest. I never mention the boy's name in this house since the funeral but just like a woman you just talk and talk and always call his name.

AWILDA: LINUS IS NOT DEAD. I remember him. Every part. I remember his scalp, his bones, his smooth flesh, the bright color of his blood, his white teeth, his boy smell. As long as I remember him, Linus is alive.

ACTS: Linus is dead. *(Taking her in his arms)* But I'm here.

AWILDA: *(Pushing him away)* If Linus could run as fast as you did, he could be here too.

(ACTS *recoils from her as if she had slapped him.*)

AWILDA: (*Horrified at what has slipped out of her mouth*) "He that is cruel troubleth his own flesh." Book of Proverbs, 29th Chapter, 11th verse. I feel terrible. I hope you can forgive me.

ACTS: (*Returning to his car*) You know a junkyard is a funny place. Most of the cars are thrown in the scrapheap because of lots of wear and tear. Not because they are worthless. Not worthless at all.

AWILDA: Forgive me. It's just that we used to have two boys and now there's only one.

(ACTS' *only response is the voice of his hammer.*)

AWILDA: And that one floats around with a bomb in his heart.

(ACTS *continues to pound away.*)

AWILDA: While I dream of Linus every night.

(ACTS' *hammer continues to be his only response.*)

AWILDA: I did it again last night.

(ACTS' *hammering begins to accelerate.*)

AWILDA: The only way I can remember it is to tell it.

(ACTS *continues to hammer away.*)

AWILDA: It's always the same dream. Linus is still ten years old but yet he is older than all of us. You and Linus and I are strolling down the avenue. Suddenly, Aretha's voice is all around us. We breathe it in with our bodies. It is like a feeding. When all of a sudden the music changes and the sound of Monk's piano jumps in front of us. The boy and I jump into the chords, leaving our bodies like old clothes.

(ACTS *stops working on the car, looks at her as if this is the first time he has ever heard this.*)

AWILDA: A-n-d you...you steal our bodies and run!

ACTS: I do not! I DO NOT!

AWILDA: You run and run and run and run! (*In the voice of Linus*) "Daddy, Daddy. Please...don't...run."

ACTS: (*Yelling and screaming*) You are such a liar! Look at you with your face twisted like a peach pit. You are such a liar! If lies were brains you'd be smart. If lies were mountaintops you'd be way up. If I wasn't such a calm and gentle man I'd strangle you till you admit that I don't run away. That I rush to your side. That I put your bodies in mine. I keep telling you that.

AWILDA: I know. Maybe I'll get it right tonight.

ACTS: If you could only go to sleep thinking, "He could never run away and leave us in danger."

AWILDA: But when I'm awake, I tell you that I believe you. Besides, what do you care what I think as long as God knows the truth. Isn't God enough for you?

ACTS: HELL NO! I need people. I need you. There are nights when I see myself all the way to my bones. Check out every corner of myself and feel strong about me. But come the morning...I look at you and the doubt I see in you makes me guilty.

AWILDA: "Heal me O Lord, my bones are vexed. My soul is sore vexed." Clean my thoughts and keep the Devil out of them. I want to believe you. I have to believe you but...but...just give me another chance. I'll dream it right. I promise. I'll wake myself up if I dream it wrong.

ACTS: All of us have a dream world. Get in, my lady.

(*Reluctantly,* AWILDA *climbs in the frame of the car and sits. He continues in the manner of a king showing his queen the castle.*)

ACTS: This is where the radio's gonna be. Soon you'll be able to flick the dial to your favorite music. Not

none of them Jesus songs, honey. I mean give me a
break. You should learn how to drive. Be good for
you. Give you something else to think about. You
comfortable? I'm gonna cover the seats with something
soft. Mink maybe. Just for you. Gonna put a bar
in the back. You can keep your ginger ale in there.
If you want. Here we go sweetcakes. Past Jamaica
Avenue. Mmmmmmmmm. Smell the air. Someone's
barbecuing. On. Here we go. We're cruising up
past Kissena Boulevard, down Sunset, past Jamaica
Avenue. Mmmmmmmmmmm. Smell the air. Someone's
barbecuing. Look at those old wooden frame houses
next to the tall apartment buildings. See the churches.
See the ladies in they pinks and yellows and whites
and blues. See the folks hanging out. See them turn
they heads as we go riding by. Whew! Hot, isn't it?
Let's get a couple of beers and drive out to the beach,
take off our clothes, and lay in the sun—

AWILDA: *(Standing up, breaking the spell)* I'm late for
church.

ACTS: Shh. Don't be scared. Don't be nervous. You with
me now. Sit back down!

AWILDA: *(Sitting down)* I can't help it.

ACTS: I know. I know. Just get it together. Listen, don't
you hear what people are saying? They are saying,
"There goes the wizard of the automobile world. Acts
Benjamin and his wife. See that car he's driving? He
only builds them for the leading citizens of the world."

(ACTS sees AWILDA getting up and tries to pull her back)

ACTS: Hey, where are you going? We're almost there.
I'll park the car and we can lay in the sun—

AWILDA: I want to get out. I need my white gloves! I'm
late for church!

ACTS: It's folks like you that give religion a bad name.

AWILDA: *(Escaping from the car)* Now you listen to me.
I'd rather do what God tells me than listen to you.
(Resuming her search for gloves) All you do is rummage
through junkyards, bringing scrap that been thrown
away right here, in our living room, working on the
car, in our living room, every hour, day or night,
winter or summer, snowstorm or heatwave, in our
living room!

ACTS: That's just why I want it in the house—so that
the weather don't matter.

AWILDA: All the time, whacking, banging, drilling on
that...that....

ACTS: Car...it's a car. I've told you two hundred times
before. Don't call my car out of its name. Please...
don't...badmouth...my...car...!

AWILDA: All the time working on that car. Something
I always wanted to ask you. Tell me. Just what do you
get out of it? What do you see in it?

ACTS: Anything I want to.

AWILDA: Just tell me what.

ACTS: I'm glad you finally asked. When I look at this
car I see lots of things.

AWILDA: What things?

ACTS: I see understanding. No worries. I see tittie-
squeezing and pussy-teasing.

AWILDA: It's no wonder that I turned to Christ.

ACTS: No wonder.

AWILDA: Pastor says that you....

ACTS: If I didn't have first-hand personal knowledge
that Jesus done locked your thighs and thrown the key
away, that religion done stole your natural feelings, I'd

be 'clined to think that you and that jackleg son of a
bi—

AWILDA: *(With religious fervor)* Jealous. That's what you
are. Just plain jealous. Imagine being jealous of God.
That's why you badmouth the messengers of God's
word every chance you get. I used to have a hard heart
like you till Pastor saved me. One day I was listening
to him preach, my breath grew short, my throat closed
up, and I couldn't breathe. It was Pastor Delroy I was
looking at but Jesus that I was seeing. "Lord," I said.
"Lord, I am in your hands."

(AWILDA's *fervor has aroused* ACTS. *He goes toward her
and seriously tries to possess her. She struggles hard.)*

ACTS: I was once into that holiness bag and I know
that trick. All them jackleg pastors and deacons and
elders laughing at you and taking your money. All you
women jumping up and down yelling, "Come sweet
Jesus" need to stay home and say it to your husbands!

AWILDA: You ain't nothing but the Devil!

ACTS: *(Suddenly disgusted, walks away from her, laughing
harshly)* Forget about the Devil. Forget about the sign of
the Cross. It is the sign of power *(Holds up a dollar bill)*
and the sign of the trick *(Holds up a pair of soiled white
gloves in the other hand)* that counts.

AWILDA: You! You had them all the time.

ACTS: *(Returning to work on his car)* Maybe.

AWILDA: *(Snatching up the white gloves)* These white
gloves are genuine brushed cotton. The other day I was
downtown window-shopping, thinking about what
I would wear in church today and suddenly I found
myself in Bonwit's. I don't know how I got there. It
was like my feet had grown a mind of they own. I
wanted to turn around and run but something made
me brazen it out. So I marched to the glove counter and

stood there. Four detectives followed me. The salesgirl
left the blue-haired, silver-foxed madame she was
waiting on and rushed over to me. "Can I help you,
Miss," she said. Imagine that. "Miss" to me though I
am a married woman and had — at one time — two
children. Then I told her, "I'm not a Miss, I'm a Mrs,
and I'd like a pair of white gloves." "They start at fifty
dollars, Miss," she snapped. And then I took my time
and made her show me lace gloves, net gloves, nylon
gloves, leather gloves, and I didn't like any of them
until she showed me these. The most expensive ones
and I said, "Oh, aren't they lovely. I'll take them." And
so after all that aggravation I don't see why you would
hide them from me unless you wanted to make me late
for church and keep me here with you.

ACTS: *(Working on the car)* I'm getting kinda hungry,
woman.

AWILDA: Sure. What would you like. Spark plugs?
Machine oil? Gasoline? *(ACTS ignores her.)* I really think
sometimes that you are turning into that car.

ACTS: Honk honk!

AWILDA: You could come with me if you wanted to.
You could get dressed and come with me to church.

ACTS: Don't get started on that again. Please.

AWILDA: *(Going toward the windows)* I'm opening up all
the windows.

ACTS: *(Preoccupied)* Yeah, yeah, yeah, yeah.

AWILDA: Every night I lay out your striped blue
suit and your Van Heusen shirt with the rolled
collar and your diamond stick pin and your patent-
leather wing tips and your ribbed silk socks and
your monogrammed hand-embroidered linen pocket
handkerchief hoping that you will come to church with
me.

ACTS: Me? I keep telling you. I don't go for that bull. Besides, your beloved Pastor is there. You don't need me.

AWILDA: Need? I need you to talk to me. What happened that night....Tell me that. That's what I need.

(Silence. ACTS works on the car.)

AWILDA: See that? All the trouble we went through was for God but all you think about is that car. You can build me a Rolls Royce and say it's mine but it ain't. It's God's car.

(The sound of ACTS working is his only response.)

AWILDA: Mister Benjamin. I'm a God-fearing woman and I'm opening all these windows wide so that He can come in here and fill your heart.

ACTS: *(Looking up from his car)* Stay away from the windows.

AWILDA: *(Running around, opening up windows)* Get him God. Get him God. Come in. Come in. Stab his soul. Pierce his stubborn heart!

ACTS: *(Enraged, runs around slamming windows)* Shutupshutupshutup. Goddammit! *(He smashes all the windows with a tool.)*

AWILDA: *(Singing at the top of her voice)* I knit my world With strong church yarn With stitches even and unbroken For God is my true husband Who keeps me from harm He is my only one.

(As ACTS finishes breaking the windows, they gaze at each other silently. The maniacal peal of church bells rushes through the broken window. AWILDA goes over to the mantelpiece, fighting tears, tries to light a candle but the wind from the broken window keeps extinguishing it.)

AWILDA: Blue is for peace.

(ACTS stands there gazing at the broken glass.)

AWILDA: I...we...need a blue candle.

ACTS: *(Looking at the broken windows and glass)* I'll clean it up later. I'm going to finish that car tonight. *(Returns to car)*

AWILDA: We've got to take care of one another. Keep healthy. There's no one else to look after us. *(Begins a frantic search for something)* Where is it? I know I put it here.

ACTS: Where is what? You got the white gloves, don't you?

AWILDA: YOU KNOW what I'm looking for.

ACTS: I don't have anything to do with it. Ever since it come in the mail yesterday, I give it to you.

AWILDA: I couldn't look at it. But I remember. I put it right here.

ACTS: Then that's where it should be.

AWILDA: It's not.

ACTS: It should be right where you put it.

AWILDA: It isn't.

ACTS: Look. If it can't walk, if it ain't got legs of it own, then it's gotta be where you put it.

AWILDA: *(Discovering a check)* Aha! Here it is. And I didn't put it there. Why do you keep doing that?

ACTS: What? Doing what?

AWILDA: The check. Putting it near my candles. This is the second time I've moved it away from here.

ACTS: I don't. I didn't.

AWILDA: Then how did it get here next to my candles?

ACTS: Don't ask me.

AWILDA: *(Gingerly taking up check and looking at it)* UGH. I hate to touch it. It feels...funny. It's got an awful

smell too. It must be the paper they use nowadays to
print these things. "Payment for Wrongful Death." Big
digits. Now we got lots of money. Lots of money for
the life of our boy. How do they figger? How do they
know? How do they add up what a ten-year-old boy's
life is worth to his parents? Maybe they have a chart
or something. Probably feed it into a computer. Bzzzz.
One scrawny brown working-class boy. Enter. No
wealthy relatives. Size four shoe. A chance of becoming
rich in his lifetime if he plays Lotto regularly. How
many dollars? How many cents? Do they know about
the time I found out I was pregnant with him? My
absolute joy that God has sent me this child. True, I
already had Walter but that was before you. But you
loved us anyhow and soon Linus was growing inside
of me because we were in love. Yes, there was never
enough money and we were always struggling but
that's just the way life is. We knew we were supposed
to have this baby. You took me to your mother and
father and sisters and all your sisters, brothers, aunts,
and uncles. Your whole tribe. You told them, "This is
my woman and she's going to have our child." They all
hugged and kissed me. Do they know about the way
you would put your head on my stomach and listen?
Did they figger in the way you held my hand with
tears in your eyes when I was in labor? When he was
born the grandparents, aunts, uncles, neighbors, and
friends brought presents, ate and drank and danced
and sang. Do they know about those moments? Did
they add them in here? And what about Linus himself?
He would make me throw out all my mean, petty,
selfish parts and give him the best person I could be.
Remember when he was good? Remember when he
was bad? The times he was like us yet someone brand-
new? And...what...about... what...he...might...have...
been? How do they figger? How do they know?

ACTS: Evil. Blood money. Payoff. Hush money.... Do what you want with it and don't tell me.

AWILDA: No one could fault you if you put it in the bank or started your own something with it. Every worldly person has got some fantasy.

(ACTS *glares angrily at her but doesn't answer.*)

AWILDA: I understand. If you would only talk about that night. Tell someone what really happened. Somebody. Anybody. Especially me.

(ACTS *continues to remain silent.*)

AWILDA: One thing for sure. It ain't ordinary money and I won't buy a car or a house or store up riches like a vain, greedy sinner.

ACTS: *(Barely audible)* I tried to protect him.

AWILDA: *(Does not hear ACTS and continues)* I thought Walter would have taken over after Linus. Look after everything. Look after us...after "the accident" I put all my hopes on Walter. He was always making something. He was smart! He was kind! He was tender! You remember?

(ACTS *holds* AWILDA.)

AWILDA: Now he's got a grenade for a soul. Guns. Knives. Before the "accident" there wasn't a mean bone in his body. He loved everybody. Everybody loved him. He used to sing and dance and laugh all the time. You remember?

ACTS: Go to church. I think a storm is coming.

AWILDA: *(Holding her arms as if cradling a child, singing a lullaby)* Go to sleep my little son. Snow is falling on the sun. Trees run blood and sidewalks grow Guns besides a dead boy child! *(Suddenly walking away from* ACTS*)* Don't worry about a storm. The sun will light my path all the way to church. When I get there I will just pay attention to the songs and sermons, the music and words, voices, faces and feelings that keep me going. I guess I just believe in spiritual things. Spiritual things is all.

ACTS: Better go. It's getting late.

AWILDA: *(Whirling around dervishlike in her agony)* Then you stop time. I want you to stop it. Stop...time...now. Turn time back in its track. Make time go back to when Linus was alive. Make time go back to when Walter was tender. He was gentle. He wouldn't hurt anybody. Turn back time! Stop! Time! Stop!

(During AWILDA's *monologue,* BLOOD *has stuck his face through one of the broken windows. While she is still speaking, he surreptitiously climbs through the window, registering fear and confusion.)*

BLOOD: *(At first in the voice of a terrified little child)* Mommy? Daddy? What's wrong? What happened? You aren't hurt are you? O GOD! MA? POPS? *(Guns drawn, searching for imagined invaders)* ALL RIGHT. WHOEVER YOU ARE I KNOW YOU ARE HIDING IN THIS HOUSE. I KNOW YOU ARE HERE SOMEWHERE IN HERE. THROW OUT YOUR WEAPONS. GIVE YOURSELF UP. 'CAUSE I CAN BOMB YOU, SHOOT YOU, OR CUT YOU. I DONE WARNED I AIN'T NO PUNK YOU DEALING WITH. THIS IS ME. BLOOD! *(He stalks around the room, searching for enemies.)* Come on out. YA STUPID PUNK BASTIDS. I GOT YA COVERED FROM EVERY ANGLE. I WANT YOU ALIVE BUT I HAVE ENUF TO BLAST YA OUT! BETTER COME ON OUT NOW 'CAUSE YOU FOOLING WITH A MAN WHO IS NOT AFRAID OF DEATH!

ACTS: FUCK YOU! This is our home. Put that gun down!

AWILDA: This is our home!

BLOOD: *(Continuing his search)* I'LL BREAK YOUR
NECKS. I'LL SMASH YOUR HEADS! I'LL BREAK
YOUR BACKS!

AWILDA: Walter! *(To* ACTS*)* Look at him! Imagine being
afraid of my own son!

BLOOD: It's okay Ma. Don't be afraid. COME ON OUT,
GUYS. YOU DON'T HAVE A CHANCE!

ACTS: Give...me...the...gun, Walter.

BLOOD: GIVE IT UP! COME ON OUT! IT'S ALL OVER.
I'LL BUST YOUR HEADS!

AWILDA: A killer ain't a pretty sight.

BLOOD: SHOW YOURSELVES NOW. HOW MANY OF
THEM DID YOU SAY THERE ARE, POPS?

ACTS: There's nobody in the house but us, punk, so...
give...me...the gun!

BLOOD: I'LL BLOW UP EVERY CORNER OF THIS
HOUSE TILL THEY COME OUT WITH THEIR
HANDS UP!

*(*ACTS *has sneaked behind* BLOOD*. He knocks him down and
gets the gun.)*

ACTS: *(Pressing the gun right to* BLOOD's *head)* You
want to play crazy? I'll show you how! This is the
lowdownest trick you've pulled yet. This tops all!

BLOOD: You just can't sneak up from behind, knock me
on the floor, and take my piece.

ACTS: I can't?

BLOOD: You'd better give it back to me before I get
mad.

ACTS: You will?

AWILDA: *(To* BLOOD, *in a soft, terrified voice; she keeps on
repeating the words underneath the following dialogue.)*

Don't run don't shoot don't run don't shoot don't run don't shoot.

ACTS: *(Touches* AWILDA *to reassure her)* Will snookums get soooo maddy mad and doo-doo all over hims diapers? SHITFACE. YA FUCKING DUMB-ASS KID.

BLOOD: I'M NOT A KID. I'M A MAN.

ACTS: Didn't I tell you to keep your behind parts away from here `til you could stop acting like a hysterical female. Like a lady on the ra—

BLOOD: I'M NO LADY, MISTER. I'M A MAN!

ACTS: *(Keeping the gun aimed at his head)* Then stand up...M-A-N.

BLOOD: Why you putting that pistol at me? I'm your son.

ACTS: Get up!

BLOOD: *(Getting up)* Listen to me. Quit pointing it at me. It's loaded. You never listen.

ACTS: You busted into my house with a loaded gun and you want me to listen. Go ahead. Talk!

BLOOD: I...I...just came to say goodbye.

ACTS: *(Pressing the gun right up against* BLOOD's *temple)* Damn right you gonna say "goodbye".

BLOOD: Easy. It's loaded. Let me explain.

ACTS: Speak, liar.

BLOOD: When I opened my eyes this morning I got that old feeling again. As I lay in my room, on my bed, I could see Linus' blood on every street. The chalk outline of his body on every corner. I could see his brown leather jacket and his baseball cap tipped to the side. Once again this city was getting to me. I had to split. As I was coming down the street, walking to this house, I practiced saying goodbye. I knew you

would be working on the car and when I told you I
was leaving again you would grunt but not look at
me. Mom would light a candle for me and look at me,
accusing me, but not saying anything. As I come near
the house I sense something isn't right. I creep up on
the porch, afraid of my own eyes. Windows are busted.
I hear Mom's voice. What's she saying? Sounds like
crying. You are standing. Just standing in a river of
broken glass. Staring. Staring out a busted window.
What am I supposed to think? I stare in, thinking,
"Don't worry, Pops. Your son's here. I'll protect you."

ACTS: Well, well, well. You protect me? What we
have here is mighty Robin Hood. All you need is your
pointed, upturned ballet slippers and your green
tights!

BLOOD: It's the truth.

ACTS: You're a liar and this (*Indicating gun*) is a lie.

(BLOOD *just shakes his head from side to side.*)

ACTS: Never play with guns. Even if they aren't loaded.
Didn't I always teach you that?

BLOOD: You wanna kill me Pops? It's loaded.

ACTS: Liar!

BLOOD: Believe me. It is.

(ACTS *pulls the trigger. It clicks empty. He looks at* BLOOD
with disgust and throws the empty gun at his feet.)

ACTS: Get that thing away from around me!

BLOOD: (*Pleadingly*) So it wasn't loaded. Aren't you the
one that always says, "Attitude is everything, Son"?

ACTS: A bellowing bull never gets fat.

BLOOD: (*Walking and talking like a tough-guy gangster
type*) You gotta be hard. Tough. Cold. Ice. Steel. Woof

or be woofed at. Take no shit. Play with death. Learn to gamble. Learn to win. Learn to kill.

AWILDA: Your brother wouldn't like to see you act this way. Especially today. Have some respect. I thought you were going to kill us.

BLOOD: You afraid of me? O my God, Mom. I could never hurt you.

AWILDA: *(Begins to sweep the broken glass)* I mean there's all kinds of other ways to enter a house. You could have knocked on the door. Rang the bell...come through the front door.... A lot of other ways.

BLOOD: I'm sorry.

AWILDA: I remember the time you smashed the blue Mercury into the plate-glass window of Mister Johnny's barber shop. Your father straightened out the motor bed, plugged the holes in the radiator, hammered out some of the dents and folds in the fender, and taped a new light onto its front. It was one of the few times you helped him. Linus was always working on cars with him but you hardly did. You were different.

BLOOD: *(Taking broom from* AWILDA*)* You shouldn't do that. I'll do it.

AWILDA: *(Exiting)* Pastor's waiting for me. I'm late for church.

BLOOD: *(Goes over to* ACTS*)* Isn't there anything you can do?

ACTS: *(Working on the car)* Do? About what?

BLOOD: Can't you get her away from that holy hustler? Can't you stop her from always going crosstown to his so-called "church"?

ACTS: I tried, Walter.

BLOOD: I keep telling you the name is "Blood."

(Almost unconsciously, without being told, BLOOD *begins to hand* ACTS *tools that he needs. They pass the tools between them like a surgical team during the following monologue.)*

ACTS: I know why you doing all this. I know. I know why you so set to hurt me. It's your doubt about that night. Something you can never bring yourself to tell me. But the thought is always in you. I see it. I catch you looking at me wondering...and then turning away when I look at you. You think what people say about that night is true. I knew that soon as you went and changed your name. That wasn't right. You and I was real tight. Closer than father and son. We was Ace Boon Coons. 'Member the time I made a deluxe racer for you out of a rusty bicycle frame I found in the yard? We had a lot of nice years together before— Why you wanna go and call yourself "Blood" when you got a perfectly good name like Walter Acts Benjamin the Second? There's a lot that goes into a name and you shouldn't just go and call yourself something else. A name belongs in a family. It was passed down to me and I take it and give it to you even though you ain't my flesh and blood directly. And you take it and throw it away. You shouldn't do that. I remember the first time I heard how good things were in New York. I decided to see for myself. I wasn't used to the cold and almost went back home but after a while I decided to stay. The first job I had in the city was driving a cab. Then I carted coal for a couple of years. After that I worked as a longshoreman when I could. Then I went to work for a man named Quinn at the wrecking yard on Springfield Boulevard. And I worked many years as a garage handyman hoping one day to achieve the title of mechanic. I went near crazy from being alone until I met you and your ma. I first saw her in a little restaurant on South Road. The Silver Fly. I had to have her. We stayed up late talking and laughing. Soon we got married because after all that aloneness I been through she was having a kid for me. A baby with my eyes, my nose, my mouth, and my name. Now I'm telling you straight, boy, what happened to your brother is done. I can't change it. Your mother can't change it and God won't. You ain't no different from any other person that something terrible has happened to. Don't let what happened to Linus madden or cheapen you. I bear a lot of pain but I bear it with expression. Just who in the hell do you think you are?

BLOOD: (*Walks away from him*) Who am I? I want to be a righteous gunman like George Jackson. Or his brother, Jonathan. I would have liked to walk in the courtroom where they acquitted the cop that shot my brother in the back with my guns drawn and announce, "All right, gentlemen, I'm taking over." Just like Jonathan did. Alone and armed. Righteous and tough. Beyond fear. He knew his fate and did not hesitate. A man evolved to the highest level. Now they mighta shot some bullets into Jonathan Jackson's brain that day but he ain't dead. I got to be him 'cause I sure ain't me. I should be the kind of man that pours down hot revenge on his enemies because I had a brother, once. A kid brother. Sometimes he used to pee in the bed. A scrawny, ash-brown kid, ninety-four pounds, about this high. He was always beating up on little girls 'cause he liked them. Used to be afraid of being weak and afraid. We used to arm-wrestle all the time and I'd let him win and then show him how I could beat him anytime I wanted to. He looked up to me and I liked that.

ACTS: Tell you what, "Blood" or whatever you call yourself. We got some money now. Plenty of it with that "wrongful death" check from the city that come yesterday. Ask your mother for some. You'd be able to go anyplace.

BLOOD: I don't want any of that money. I can get all kinds of bread.

ACTS: Yeah?

BLOOD: Yeah.

ACTS: You called me on the phone and asked me for money, I remember.

BLOOD: That was a long time ago.

ACTS: When you gonna pay me back?

BLOOD: Soon.

ACTS: You need money. Ask your mother.

BLOOD: You think I want to stand here and argue with you about that filthy blood money? I know the price we've all paid for it.

ACTS: You sure you don't want to come sneaking up on us and knife us in the back?

BLOOD: That's not funny, Pops. I hate that money much as you. It's no treasure. It's no pot of gold after the rainbow.

(AWILDA *starts to enter and stops. Audience sees her standing and listening.* BLOOD *and* ACTS *are unaware of her presence.*)

ACTS: Money, money, money. It's the story of our lives. "Learn how to make you a dollar, boy. Earn some spending change and keep you some folding money and don't let anybody take your money from you," I used to preach to Linus. So he would get up every Saturday and go to the yard with me before dawn. That's when they shot him. Right before daybreak. And though everybody knew the truth, they said Police Officer Rhea was only doing his duty.

BLOOD: In school he would tear up his work in a rage if he got a bad mark. At home, he was our mother's favorite child and I knew it. When he discovered he had a joint he used to go around touching it, looking at it, airing it out, seeing how far he could pee with it. What a little brat!

AWILDA: *(Entering the room, concentrating on her white-gloved hands)* Pastor said Linus would have turned out to be somebody. Somebody big. You know what Pastor says. Pastor says we should give Linus a special memorial. Something unusual and unselfish. That's what Pastor says.

(Lights start to dim as AWILDA *continues to turn her hands inside out, stretching her arms toward the sky as if she were dancing.)*

AWILDA: Ever notice how when you wash white gloves just one time all the life seems to go out of them? Suddenly they are old. Like faded bits of sunlight. Can you tell these are not fresh, pure, unwashed white gloves that I'm wearing to church this morning?

END OF ACT ONE

ACT TWO

Scene One

(Evening. New windowpanes. Everything has been cleaned. BLOOD *is repairing the last window.* ACTS *is underneath his car, working.)*

BLOOD: *(Talk-singing to himself as he hammers a nail in place and plays an imagined guitar)* And I said to myself 'Cause I'm always talking to me, "Self," said I, "We all must die And darkness will soon surround us."

"Ohhhhhhhhh NO!" Self hollered, "I don't want to be dead, Me, I ain't never gonna die Gonna buy a car, Gonna drive it far, Gonna drive away from me, myself, and I."

(Steps back and surveys his work) Shall I paint them, stain them, or what?

ACTS: *(Preoccupied)* Mmmmm. Yeah. Okay...

BLOOD: Which one?

ACTS: Whatever. Valves are slightly worn but that's light stuff.

BLOOD: *(Angrily)* How would you like the windows done up in red? Red paint?

ACTS: Wrist pins and connecting rod bearings are in good condition.

BLOOD: It must be hard on Mom.

ACTS: She'll be glad you fixed them. Low oil consumption. This baby is practically brand-new.

BLOOD: I'm not talking 'bout the windows. I mean her. My mother and your wife.

ACTS: What about her? The flywheel is okay too. Hotdammit! It's gonna be something else when I finish.

BLOOD: Nothing else matters to you. That's gotta be hard on her.

ACTS: S'no difference between a car and a woman. Cool 'em. Ignite 'em. Give 'em plenty of lubrication. Keep their engine in good condition.

BLOOD: *(As he speaks he writes red graffiti on the new window panes)* I had a woman once. She worked at the express counter in the supermarket. I used to make seven, eight shopping trips a day just to walk through her line. Every time she saw me she smiled and I was sure she really loved me. Whenever she asked me if I wanted a single or double bag I knew she was really pledging her love. And all those times I replied, "Single bag, thank you" I was really asking her to let me drink her bathwater.   Although I never knew her name, we were very happy. All over the city I drew red hearts for her. No clean space went unmarked. I even added some of my blood to the red paint. When I pricked all my fingers and toes I started on my knuckles and ankles. It hurt like hell!   One time I stayed up all night making hearts for her. Next morning I ran to our supermarket and got on her line. Some man was with her making her laugh. She didn't even know that I was there. I just stood there looking at her. I screamed at her silently, "You love him and not me. You want his low voice, his strong chest, and his big thighs. Why can't you want me?" I was very angry.

ACTS: *(Surveying the windowpanes without ever stopping his work)* I know what you trying to do but it won't work. You striving to prevent me from getting my work done. You hate this car. You trying to keep it from being born. Now you can act a fool if you want but just don't get in my way.

BLOOD: *(Resignedly looking over the car)* It's state-of-the-art all right.

ACTS: Damn straight.

BLOOD: You sure ain't no "pliers-and-screwdriver" mechanic.

ACTS: Never was. Never will be.

(BLOOD *takes out a gleaming knife with a feather stuck in its handle and plays with it.)*

ACTS: What...is...that?

BLOOD: It's a knife, man.

ACTS: For what?

(BLOOD *slowly takes out an orange and begins slowly to peel it as he looks at the car.)*

BLOOD: For peeling things. I like to peel things. Just like to see if with one, slow, continuous, steady movement I can take the skin off anything in one, long, thin, graceful piece.

ACTS: Hope you can handle a knife better than you can a gun.

BLOOD: I can do a lot of things. *(Holding up the entire orange peel in one piece)*

ACTS: What about important things? You remember the first time I put you underneath a car?

BLOOD: No. I don't remember.

ACTS: You need to kneel down beside me again and take another look. Give you a different perspective when you laying on your back flat out, looking up inside the belly of a car.

BLOOD: No thanks. All you do is wake up thinking about your car and sleep dreaming about it. No thank you. What about me? You never really talk to me. And when you talk you never really say anything.

ACTS: Okay, you been after me all this time so I'm gonna talk. Gonna tell you something. So listen real good.

(*As* ACTS *speaks,* BLOOD *keeps peeling, letting the peelings and fruit pile up on the floor. Every once in a while he seems to nick himself accidentally.*)

ACTS: In this world, in order to survive, you gotta have a little gris-gris to depend on. It could be anything. A prayer, a saying, a rabbit foot, a horseshoe, a song. A way of looking at life, a way of doing things, a way of understanding the world you find yourself in. Something that will never fail to pull you through the hard times. Now I see you got no formula for survival, no magic, no juju, so let me give you a very important piece of mojo right now. Always remember that the secret of a car is its engine. The engine is the car's heart. Treat it right and you can trust it. The trick is you gotta take your time and learn it. Study it inside out. Most folks abuse the engine by racing it when it's cold. How would you like to be waked up in the morning by someone shouting and screaming at you while you're still yawning and under the covers? You couldn't respond even if you wanted to. It takes time to fully warm up. And you gotta give it good fuel. Then you gotta inspire it. Set it on fire. Ignite the bad boy. Then he's gotta be stroked and lubricated real good. Now don't forget there's plenty of fire and heat inside so you gotta cool him off, too. Learn the engine, boy. Understand the heart. It's the secret of life.

BLOOD: Is that all you can talk about? Cars? Is that all?

ACTS: Fool! Is that all you think I'm talking about? *(He grimaces in sudden pain.)*

BLOOD: What is it...what's wrong?

ACTS: *(A gesture of weariness)* Nothing. I ache all over.

BLOOD: What do you expect, hunched over that car all day and night? A good massage will fix you up. *(He begins to massage* ACTS' *shoulders, gently at first, and then with increasing violence.)*

ACTS: Ahhhhhh. That feels good. Ouch. Not so rough.

(A look passes between BLOOD *and* ACTS *which establishes the element of distrust between them.)*

BLOOD: *(Continuing the massage)* Is this where the pain is? *(Gives him a powerful whack on his shoulders)*

ACTS: *(Trying unsuccessfully to move away from him)* No! Get away from me.

BLOOD: *(Trying to continue massage)* Be still.

ACTS: Kinda rough there, aren't you, "Blood"?

BLOOD: *(Poking* ACTS*)* Is the pain here? Or there?

ACTS: Let me go! Ouch! Ow!

(Another look passes between them.)

BLOOD: Oh, I'm sorry, man.

ACTS: Walter, don't you know when you're hurting someone?

BLOOD: I'm not sure what you want, Dad.

ACTS: I want you to stop, Son.

BLOOD: *(Gives* ACTS *a final, painful shoulder jab)* There! Doesn't that feel better?

ACTS: Holy shit. What the hell is going on here?

BLOOD: Every movement, every touch means something. *(Suddenly releasing* ACTS *and running toward the car)*

ACTS: Get back. Don't touch it. Keep away.

BLOOD: It's a beautiful car. Just beautiful. *(He begins to disarrange various parts of the car.)*

ACTS: That's not it! That's not it at all! Get away from the damn thing. Stand back. *(Pushing* BLOOD *away from the car)* Just look at it and don't touch a damn thing!

*(*BLOOD *stands for several beats, looking at the car. He holds his hands together as if in prayer. Then he suddenly begins to pick up the peelings and fruit from the floor and carries them to* AWILDA's *candles on the mantelpiece, where he spreads them while mumbling in a strange language.* ACTS *watches him, fascinated.)*

BLOOD: It's a ritual.

ACTS: Ritual?

BLOOD: Yes. For your forgiveness.

ACTS: Mine?

BLOOD: Yes.

ACTS: Why?

BLOOD: *(Searching)* Because...because...you broke the windows! WHY DID YOU BREAK THEM?

ACTS: That was because your mother started on me about her "Pastor." I went off. The ground parted. Quick flashes of lightning stabbed at my head. My blood boiled.

BLOOD: I know the feeling.

ACTS: Be careful. It's in our blood.

BLOOD: What's it called?

ACTS: It ain't a disease. It's a condition. A condition
I tell you. All of us are thinking about one thing. A
boy brought up in the city and killed by wild dogs.
(Returning to his car) But when I am working on this car
I don't feel a thing. I feel clean. I feel strong. I feel free.

BLOOD: I feel like shit!

ACTS: Get away from your mother's candles.

BLOOD: My mother! What do you care about her?

ACTS: I do. A lot. But she's with her "Pastor" now.

BLOOD: *(Exploding, violently blowing out candles)* Shit
on her Pastor! *(Blows out more candles)* To hell with his
so-called church! *(Blows out some more candles)* I hate
Sunday con men! *(Blows out the last candles)* And their
wicked trickerations!

ACTS: Don't do that! What gives you the right?

BLOOD: Pops, let's leave here. Let's not stay here. We
should just take that money and run. You and me and
Mom should get outta this place. Make a new start.

ACTS: Oh yeah? Where, for instance?

BLOOD: Let's go to Mexico.

ACTS: Mexico? What they got down there for me
besides refried beans and the worthless peso?

BLOOD: You could get land cheap down there. In less
than ten years it's worth three times what you paid.
You could build cars down there. I know a special spot
down there. A city in the mountains.

ACTS: That's your world. My world is right here. A
world where all the cars that my mind can conjure up
is brought to life.

BLOOD: Forget it man.

ACTS: So...you liked it down in Mexico.

BLOOD: I didn't get in trouble with the police if that's what you mean.

ACTS: Then why did you come back this time?

BLOOD: We're family. We're chained together.

ACTS: Then why are you leaving?

BLOOD: I can't stay here. Do you know what it means to be the surviving brother? You never talk about the morning that Linus was killed. You were with him when he got killed but you don't tell what really happened.

ACTS: You know Walter, you'll be okay once you get yourself together. Take care of your own self. You need to get a mojo and don't worry about me none. The right mojo will give you the sayso. Put you in the driver's seat. The right mojo will take you over those moments of terror, doubt or even surprise. Nothing surprises me no more. I'm ready to take it all on.

(At this moment we hear the singing, talking, and laughing voices of AWILDA *and* PASTOR DELROY *offstage. Blackout.)*

Scene Two

(The stage slowly lights up as AWILDA *and* PASTOR *enter the room, still singing.* AWILDA, *radiant and nervous as a young girl on a date, is carrying a bouquet of multicolored gladioli.* PASTOR *wears a clerical collar, robe, and white gloves.)*

AWILDA: Mister Benjamin! Walter! You two, we have special company. Oh Pastor, what a voice you have. Deep and rich and full like a...a...man! You could have been a singer with millions of fans instead of a man of God. In church I can hear your voice over all the others. *(To* BLOOD *and* ACTS*)* What a lovely service. You two should have been there. Going to church is like going to a garden where beautiful music grows. And the beautiful carnations and gladiolas on the altar. I brought some home because church flowers are special.

PASTOR: Brothers Benjamin, senior and junior. Peace and love. Our lovely sister Awilda asked me to stop by.

ACTS: Oh yeah?

PASTOR: I see you are still working on your car? Imagine that. Looks like you'll even be finished soon. *(Makes a gesture to touch the car)*

ACTS: *(Ferociously)* Don't touch him.

PASTOR: *(Backing away, frightened)* Brother Acts. I've always felt that you fear me. There is no need to. Don't you know that "He that feareth is not made perfect in love"?

ACTS: Don't you know that he that fucketh around with my car will be made perfect in death?

PASTOR: Brother Benjamin, you can't mean that I'm not welcome here?

ACTS: You never had any trouble feeling comfortable before. The wife seems to fry chicken just the way you like it.

PASTOR: You don't expect me to refuse the gracious invitations of the lovely saints of my congregation, do you?

ACTS: I have a line in my mind that divides the killer beast from the gentle man. Be careful. You are stepping awfully near the edge.

AWILDA: There's something wrong in here. I felt it as soon as I walked in. New windows? All written over in red paint, AND WHAT IS THIS SHIT AROUND MY CANDLES? Who blew them out? What the devil is going on around here now?

BLOOD: *(Going toward her, trying to calm her)* Easy Ma, let me explain.

AWILDA: *(Shrinking back from him)* That's all right. I should have known. Every time you're around I never know what is going to happen.

BLOOD: I'll...I'll scrub the paint off...before I split.

AWILDA: No! Don't leave. Today is Linus' anniversary.

BLOOD: LINUS IS DEAD!

(AWILDA is lighting all the candles as if to revive him.)

PASTOR: Sister, do not despair. Linus is near us, though unseen. His spirit depends on us to remember him in special ways.

ACTS: Back off, Delroy! You are stepping on my line.

PASTOR: I feel Linus nearer and nearer. Sometimes I can see him. I can see him standing large as life in front of me. He never looks at me. He's just there.

BLOOD: *(To AWILDA)* Can't you see it's just an act?

PASTOR: I tell you sister, there is no death. "The stars go down to rise upon some fairer shore. And bright in heaven's jeweled crown they shine, for evermore!"

ACTS: *(Grabbing him)* You have just crossed the equator. Get the hell out!

AWILDA: Pastor should be here.

BLOOD: I'm sorry about the windows. I was only trying to communicate with my father.

AWILDA: I wanted Pastor here when I told you about the money.

PASTOR: Amen.

ACTS: What...about...the...money?

AWILDA: Linus is getting a memorial.

PASTOR: Praise Him!

BLOOD: It's a damn shame.

AWILDA: What are you saying?

BLOOD: It's a damn shame that I'm alive and Linus
isn't.

PASTOR: I tell you all that Linus is alive and we must
remember him.

ACTS: We need to be alone right now, Delroy.

AWILDA: No.

PASTOR: (*Seductively*) Awilda.

ACTS: Awilda, Awilda, now you listen. I been thinking.
This car is gonna be finished soon. Then we gonna
leave. All of us. We gonna slip out easy like a soft
wind. When folks catch on that ain't nobody in this
house anymore you know what they gonna do?
They gonna break in and I leave everything to all
of them. My rubber galoshes, my old brown leather
longshoremen's jacket with the lamb's-wool lining, my
checkerboard, my dreambooks, my fishing poles—I'll
get new ones—my Gene Ammon's seventy-eights and
my tools. Let them take my acetylene torch, cutters,
dollies and hammers, my balancers and hydraulic
pressers, my reamers, hones and wrenchers, my
gauges and gappers, and place them in the middle of
Springfield Boulevard and burn them! Any second,
this car will be finished and we'll all get in. I want you
to put on the blue dress you was wearing at the Silver
Fly that day I first seen you. And Walter's gonna wear
his Mexican shirt. The car radio's gonna be on. The
dial will be set. Chuck Berry, Ivory Joe Hunter and
Nat King Cole will be bluesing around. Little Esther
is wanting a "Sunday Kind of Love." Jimmy Garrison
is on bass. Max is on drums. Monk is on piano. The
Orioles. The Moonglows. Little Willie John and Aretha.

All the sounds of all the ages coming together in my car.

AWILDA: I remember how I used to love driving with you, listening to music, feeling the wind against my cheeks.

PASTOR: Seek ye not the vain pleasures of this world, Sister. Remember Linus.

AWILDA: Ever since the money came I been thinking. We need something money can't buy. That's why I...I...

PASTOR: You want me to hold your hand while you tell them?

AWILDA: No.

PASTOR: You want me to tell them for you?

AWILDA: No.

PASTOR: All right, then tell them!

AWILDA: I'm giving the money to Pastor's church in Linus' name.

PASTOR: Amen.

(ACTS *begins a slow, dangerous laugh.*)

PASTOR: There is no greater memorial.

(ACTS *lunges at* PASTOR *and narrowly misses him.*)

PASTOR: (*Remaining calm as he sidesteps* ACTS *and speaks in a soft, sanctimonious voice, full of righteous piety*) "He delivereth me from my enemies. Yea, from those that rise up against me. Verily I say unto you, `He delivereth me from the violent man.'" My poor, sinful brethren. You are consumed with hypocrisy and greed. "And the greedy man shall retch up his desire for it is an unclean thing." And the hypocrites shall burn! burn! in the lower depths. Rise! Cleanse yourselves and admit that you want that money. You don't want God

to have it. You lust after each dollar and have silent
plans how to spend every cent.
Remember, beloved, "Lying lips are an abomination
and the liars shall all be stripped of their foul
pretense." Why do you denounce my church? Why
do you rail against my religion? Why do you attack all
that is upright and righteous in this ungodly world full
of evil fornicators? Why do you attack me?
My only concern is Linus and his immortality. Do
not let the world forget him. He who was crushed
by the forces of wickedness! He who was the fairest
among boys. He who was snatched from us before
the soft down of manhood kissed his cheeks. His loins
yet girded with innocence. A bright-eyed, graceful
manchild. O! Countless are the splendors of this world
but none more splendiferous than was that fine, tender
young boy.

BLOOD: *(Taking out his knife)* You weren't counting on
murder, were you?

PASTOR: Perhaps you're right. I'll just come back some
other time.

(PASTOR tries to leave; BLOOD stops him with the knife.)

AWILDA: Walter, stop it. I've been so afraid that you
would hurt someone.

ACTS: *(Moving toward AWILDA)* Walter, put the knife
away. I keep telling you, it's not a mojo.

BLOOD: I have got to find a way to make you all listen
to me.

(Everyone is frozen.)

BLOOD: I've got to find a way to make you all LISTEN
TO ME!
Down in Mexico, in spots where I've been, some
natives have a ritual for this kind of man. They believe
in releasing the lies from his flesh. They just skin the

poor devil alive. I've seen it done and it's just like skinning a fruit. Now listen up, your righteousness. I'm a-going to take my knife and slowly cut you from your larynx to your rectum. Then I'm going to flop you on your belly and peel away your lying skin in one piece just like a new suit of clothes. Just like an orange peel.

(Everyone is terrified as BLOOD *keeps talking. He menaces* PASTOR *with the knife.)*

BLOOD: First, I'll work the skin over your skull and cut it with care so that it all comes off in one piece. Don't worry. I'll be careful when I cut around your eyes.

*(*PASTOR *emits a terrified howl.)*

BLOOD: I'll make an incision in your throat to a point midway in the calf of your leg.

ACTS: Walter.

BLOOD: I'll grab your scrotum. Or is it scrotii?

PASTOR: Oh Jesus!

BLOOD: And make an incision in each.

PASTOR: *(Doubling over in imagined pain, protecting his groin)* Ohhhhhhhhhhhhhhh.

BLOOD: *(To* PASTOR*)* STRIP!

*(*PASTOR *blinks frantically, not believing his ears.)*

AWILDA: Walter!

BLOOD: Look at him. I want you to look. You won't look at me and you can't see through him. *(To* PASTOR*)* I...said...off...with...the...clothes, holiness.

*(*PASTOR *slowly begins to remove his clerical collar, his white gloves, and his robe. Around his neck is gleaming gold jewelry. He is dressed in a silk suit and other items of luxury. He has revealed himself as a "dandy man." When he takes off his white gloves he reveals the talons of a bird*

of prey with gleaming rings around them. ACTS, BLOOD, *and* AWILDA *are amazed at first and then* ACTS *and* BLOOD *double over, convulsed with laughter.)*

AWILDA: Pastor? Pastor?

BLOOD: *(Ridiculing him in a singsong chant)* "He took Ms Johnson's money, poor old Miss Baker's Social Security, and made her throw in those diamonds he's wearing for an extra blessing."

ACTS: Wife? Is this who you trust over me?

AWILDA: *(In a daze)* No.

BLOOD: Off with your clothes, reverent Reverend.

(PASTOR continues to undress. He is wearing a jeweled G-string, S & M boots, and other suggestive clothing.)

BLOOD: "Jeanie Taylor, Diane Williams, and little Dickie Hill were disgraced by his sexual conduct. But his congregation forgave him."

AWILDA: *(Gets nearer to PASTOR and inspects every inch of him)* Take it all off. Down to the bone. I want to see it all.

(PASTOR hesitates; BLOOD menaces him.)

BLOOD: All off. You heard the lady, Holy Father.

(As PASTOR strips, he begins to take on the movements and rhythms of a vulture. He reveals a feathered body, a hook nose and webbed, claw feet. He makes vulture noises as he begins to execute broad, swooping circles around AWILDA, as if stalking his prey.)

AWILDA: *(Beating back the PASTOR/vulture as if exorcising something within her)* Scavenger! Bird of Prey! Vulture!

(AWILDA and PASTOR both turn around in circles, he stalking her, she beating him off.)

AWILDA: He has sharp eyes and a keen sense of smell. He can see dead animals from a great distance.

(AWILDA *tosses* PASTOR *her church flowers and white gloves, which he gobbles up, eating and retching at the same time.*)

AWILDA: He eats carrion, dead animals, dead things. He often vomits when feeding.

(PASTOR/*vulture begins to stalk her once more.*)

AWILDA: Drive back the unclean scavenger with living flesh. He only thrives on decay. Drive him out with living thoughts and a living heart. He only feeds on the dead. Only the living live in here. Out! Out! Out!

(PASTOR/*vulture is driven out through the window. Exhausted,* AWILDA *collapses in the arms of* ACTS *and* BLOOD.)

ACTS: Awilda.

AWILDA: Tell me what happened that night. Please.

BLOOD: Go ahead, Pops. Tell her.

ACTS: You are right, Son, I ran. I ran away.

BLOOD: What!?

ACTS: We both ran. The boy and I both ran.

(ACTS *holds the check, inspecting the look, feel of it as he talks to it. Lights dim, candle flames grow higher as* ACTS *continues.* AWILDA *and* BLOOD *listen intently, for this is the first time they have ever heard the story.*)

ACTS: It's funny how it always comes back to money. It's funny how money is supposed to explain everything and make anything all right. It was a Saturday, right before dawn, and as you know, the boy and I were on our way to the yard. Fooling around with cars is in my bones so I figure since Linus takes after me in so many ways he could learn it real good and earn a little change too. So when he turned ten, he started coming with me on Saturday mornings 'cause the rest of the week he's in school like he's supposed to

be. He was a nice boy. Very respectful. Very intelligent.
He would have been a good mechanic some day.   I
remember it was early spring but the dew made it
cold. The sky was that light purplish gray you get
right before dawn. We was both walking, not saying
too much. I guess it was just too early to be doing a
lot of talking. We walked down New York Boulevard
through the vacant lot littered with broken glass, past
the trees that rise right out of the trash and grow fifty
feet tall. Suddenly two guys with plain clothes pull up
in a plain car and yell at us, "Stop." Their car screams
to a halt. I didn't even recognize them as humans so
how should I know they was cops, creeping toward
us, hissing, "Stop, you sons of bitches," laughing and
drinking as they cursed us. Said in the papers they
was looking for two grown burglars. My little son
and I wasn't no burglars.   My wallet was bulging on
my hip. I had just gotten paid. I had it all figured out.
These drunken jokers were ordinary crooks trying to
rob me. I figured the way they were drinking I could
outrun both of them and you remember how Linus
could outrun a chicken. "Run," I commanded and
we took off. Linus shot in front of me and I was right
behind.   They didn't even chase us. A flat loud sound
ripped the air and Linus fell and instantly became
a red pool, his eyes a bright, white blank. They shot
Linus in the back. They killed him! They shot my boy!
Always, always, in my head, "Should I have stood my
ground and fought them? Was I trying to protect my
money more than Linus?" Ain't no way I could run
away and leave Linus alone, is there? LINUS RAN
AHEAD OF ME AND LEFT ME! I know that's the way
it happened. But sometimes a man can get confused
and the way something awful happens isn't always the
way you remember it. I play it back all the time in my
head and my only thought that night was to protect
Linus. At least that's the way I remember it.

(He slowly tears the check to shreds. Suddenly the car headlights are blinking, the motor is running, the horn is honking, and the radio is playing.)

AWILDA: *(Coyly)* Mister Benjamin, my blue dress is ready.

ACTS: Blue dress?

AWILDA: You know, the one I was wearing that day we first met. *(She removes her church clothes and reveals her blue dress.)*

BLOOD: *(Dancing around and singing in a Spanish accent while revealing his Mexican shirt)* No more pain, no more blood, no more pain, no more blood.

ACTS: *(Taking off his mechanic's clothes, reveals his striped blue suit, rolled-collar shirt, diamond stick pin, leather wing tips, etc.)* I did it just like I said I would. It's crashproof, with an automatic fire extinguisher, electric shift and front-wheel drive, and rear seats that rise through the sun roof. A pretty machine nine hundred times as powerful as human man. It ain't even a machine. It is a force of nature, that is what it is. The Mojo 9. Built by a man who walked through iron times and is still kicking. See, look. My eyes are clear. My skin is tight and my body well-tuned for any situation. You all should trust me. Come with me. Mojo can take us anyplace. Mojo will get you through. I'll show you how to build an engine, boy, and you won't have to worry your head about nothing. Come on. What are you two standing there for? Get in. What are you waiting for?

(ACTS, AWILDA, *and* BLOOD *all climb in the car and the Mojo is driven straight through the door.*)

END OF PLAY